STILETTO DOSSIER

C. C. PRESTON

Copyright © 2012
Pentecost Kouture™ Publications.
Dallas, TX.

Library of Congress Control Number: 2013913845

Copyright © 2012 C. C. Preston.
All rights reserved. Printed in the United States. No part of this book may be used or reproduced in any manner without written permission, except in the case of brief quotations embodied in articles and reviews.

Front Cover Illustration and Interior Illustrations, purchased and used with permission. Author Photo, Copyright © 2012 C. C. Preston.

ISBN: 0615798942
ISBN-13: 978-0-615-79894-3

To my Parents

To Trishie, and all of my Siblings

To my Godchildren

CONTENTS

Top Secret Mission   1

Directive I: 7
Stiletto Reconnaissance

Directive II: 17
Stiletto Modus Operandi

Top Secret Code   22

Top Secret Operation   25

Directive III: 61
Stiletto Surveillance

Directive IV: 181
Stiletto Rescue & Recovery

Top Secret Opulence   184

ACKNOWLEDGMENTS

Giving honor and thanks to my
Lord and Savior Jesus Christ.
I am nothing without God.

Thank you to my editors, mentors and
friends for your helpful advice
and keen insight.

Thank you to all of my teachers from
grade school to graduate school.
I appreciate all of you.

*"Charm is deceptive, and beauty does not last;
but a woman who fears the Lord
will be greatly praised."* [2]

Proverbs 31:30

Stiletto Prayer

Father God,

Please bless my entire Stiletto collection and command every pair of Stilettos to be a blessing to my feet. Always bless me to walk in Stilettos with grace, poise, style and confidence. I pray that I will always maintain my equilibrium. I shall not stumble or fall and injure myself or anyone else.

Amen

"Our lives are in his hands, and he keeps our feet from stumbling."
Psalms 66:9

STILETTO DOSSIER

Top Secret Mission

The Proverbs 31 Woman

"When she speaks, her words are wise, and she gives instructions with kindness."
Proverbs 31:26

"There are many virtuous and capable women in the world, but you surpass them all!"
Proverbs 31:29

"Reward her for all she has done. Let her deeds publicly declare her praise."
Proverbs 31:31

Stiletto Avowal

As a Proverbs 31 Woman, I vow to accurately reflect the **image** of Christ as a Godly woman, by ambulating correctly in a high-heel shoe or Stiletto with grace through **faith**.

*"**Faith** is the confidence that what we hope for will actually happen; it gives us assurance about things we cannot see."*
Hebrews 11:1

Top Secret Mission

The objective of this Top Secret Mission is to master the correct technique for ambulating gracefully in a Stiletto.

The **image** you convey, by the manner in which you walk, is how you are perceived, received and interpreted.

To accurately reflect the **image** of Christ as a Godly woman, it is essential to utilize the correct technique when walking in a high-heel shoe or Stiletto.

*"So God created human beings in his own **image**. In the **image** of God he created them; male and female he created them."*
Genesis 1:27

The Mission Begins

Four directives are given to assist you in accomplishing this mission.

- Directive I provides historical Stiletto data, measurements and words of caution.
- Directive II divulges the Top Secret Code and The Top Secret Operation.
- Directive III reveals Classified Stiletto Identities.
- Directive IV unveils instructions for Stiletto restoration, including sole and soul salvation.

"For I can do everything through Christ, who gives me strength.
Philippians 4:13

Ready, Set, Let's Go Stiletto!™

STILETTO DOSSIER

DIRECTIVE I

Stiletto Reconnaissance

Stiletto Introduction

The word Stiletto originated from the Italian root word "stilo" which means dagger.[5] A dagger is a "short, sword-like weapon."[1] The Italian root word "stilo" originated from the Latin word "stilus" meaning "pen."[5] These descriptive terms were likely used to name the original Stiletto high-heel shoe, due to its design, which included the insertion of a cylindrical metal rod, resembling a pen, into the high-heel. This allowed it to bear more weight.[4] There is some historical debate as to who actually invented the fashionable Stiletto high-heel. Roger Vivier (1907-1998) was a gifted designer and Parisian shop owner in the 1930's.[3] By the 1950's, he was a regaled shoe designer in the fashion house of Christian Dior.[4] Roger Vivier is credited with inventing the Stiletto high-heel.[4]

Stiletto Myth

Contrary to what some may believe, the Stiletto high-heel was not created for any illicit or immoral purposes. Nor is it a representation of such. This myth is hereby debunked. The Stiletto was created as a luxury foot adornment to express affluent style and to augment haute couture.

Stiletto Caution

In recent years, there has been some controversy about the alleged risk of bodily injury that may occur by wearing Stilettos. Follow the advice of your podiatrist and your primary care physician.

You may visit the website for the American Podiatric Medical Association to learn more about foot health and to find a podiatrist in your local area. Please use cautionary judgment when deciding to purchase or don Stilettos.

Operating an automobile while wearing Stilettos may cause friction damage to your Stilettos. Utilize caution while driving in Stilettos and use floor mats with a built-in heel pad when possible. One final word of caution . . . don Stilettos at your own risk. The risk of looking glam that is! Let's Go Stiletto!™

Stiletto Measurements

For our descriptive purposes, the word Stiletto will be used in reference to a high-heel shoe, with a heel of 3.0 Inches or higher. The following heel measurements are based on the interior height of the heel from the tip of the heel to the sole of the shoe.

Mid-Heel:
    2.0 Inches < 2.5 Inches

High-Heel: **Pre-Stiletto**
    2.5 Inches < 3.0 Inches

Stiletto: **Stiletto**
    3.0 Inches < 4.0 Inches

Stealth Stiletto: (heel-less)
    3.0 Inches or >

Super Stiletto: **Super Stiletto**
    4.0 Inches or >

Stiletto Acquisition

When purchasing new Stilettos, give yourself ample time to complete your new purchase process. Try on the prospective Stilettos during evening hours and walk or stand in them for a minimum of 15 minutes prior to finalizing your purchase. If time permits, take pictures of the prospective Stilettos on your feet, while sitting and standing. Give yourself a 24-hour cooling off period prior to completing your new Stiletto purchase. This will help eliminate impulse buying and buyer's remorse.

Stiletto Satchel

Pack a Stiletto satchel to carry with you or to keep in your automobile. The Stiletto satchel should contain one pair of flat shoes and one pair of 2.0 Inch Mid-Heels. Also, include foot antiperspirant powder or wipes, cushion sole inserts, blister plasters and a non-aerosol foot fragrance.

Stiletto Respite

It is very important to take a Stiletto respite, if needed, while ambulating in a Stiletto. Find a comfortable place to sit down and rest for a few moments. If possible, do not remove your Stilettos during your respite. Relax, breathe and remain calm.

DIRECTIVE II

Stiletto Modus Operandi

Stiletto Confidence

Have **faith** and believe in the power of God that dwells within you. Relax, breathe and be confident.

Believe in your ability to remain vertical, maintain your balance and gracefully ambulate in a Stiletto.

*"**Faith** is the confidence that what we hope for will actually happen; it gives us assurance about things we cannot see."*
Hebrews 11:1

Stiletto Avowal

As a Proverbs 31 Woman, I vow to master The Stiletto Glissade™, the Top Secret Code, and complete the Top Secret Operation to become a Precocious Stiletto Operative.

"The Lord says, I will guide you along the best pathway for your life. I will advise you and watch over you."
Psalm 32: 8

~ Sway ~

Top Secret Code Preamble

In preparation for the Top Secret Code, you will need shoes with heels of varying heights. Start with a pair of 2.0 Inch Mid-Heels. Next, you will need a pair of 2.5 Inch Pre-Stilettos. You will also need a pair of 3.0 Inch Stilettos and 4.0 Inch Super Stilettos.

Using a miniature tape measure, measure the height of the heel from the interior height of the heel from the tip of the heel to the sole of the shoe. This will ensure you are wearing the correct heel height. Reserve wedges and Stealth Stilettos (heel-less) for use after you have achieved the Professional Stiletto Operative™ designation.

Some of you may feel that you already know how to walk in a high-heel or Stiletto, however, there is a correct technique for walking gracefully in a Stiletto.

Top Secret Code:
The Stiletto Glissade™

The correct technique for ambulating in a Stiletto is called The Stiletto Glissade™. It is important to utilize proper technique while ambulating in a Stiletto.

The first part of your Stiletto to make contact with the surface of the floor is your heel. Next, is the ball of your foot, and thirdly is your (great) toe. At the completion of your right great toe making contact with the surface of the floor, gently sway your pelvis to the right. At the completion of your left great toe making contact with the surface of the floor, gently sway your pelvis to the left.

In coordination with The Stiletto Glissade™, your head should be facing forward, with your chin slightly elevated. Shoulders down and slightly back, they should be in alignment with your pelvis. Your chest should be convex. Your knees should be straight but not stiff or locked. Resist the urge to gaze downward while walking. Do not extend your head and neck forward in an attempt to balance yourself. Take small steps. For faster ambulation, take small steps faster. Heel, Ball, Toe ~ Sway (HBTS)

Heel, Ball, Toe ~ Sway

Stiletto Commando Rough Terrain

Maneuvering across rough terrain such as cobblestone streets, gravel and grass can be challenging. Whenever possible, avoid this type of terrain while ambulating in a Stiletto.

If walking on such rough surfaces cannot be avoided, please utilize the contents of your Stiletto satchel and downshift to a flat shoe prior to ambulating across this type of terrain. To conquer rough terrain in your Stilettos, quickly tiptoe forward, while keeping the heel of the Stiletto elevated as much as possible.

When ascending stairs in Stilettos, use only the ball and toe of your Stiletto to make contact with the surface of each stair. While descending stairs, the heel, ball and toe of your Stiletto should make contact with the surface of the stair all at once.

Top Secret Operation:
Master The Stiletto Glissade™ with 3 Steps in 30-Days

Step I
Proficient Pre-Stiletto Operative™

Step II
Professional Stiletto Operative™

Step III
Precocious Stiletto Operative™

Day 1
** 2.0 Inch Mid-Heels **

Your goal for Day 1 is a
½ hour of continuous wear.

(Preferably in the morning
on a carpeted floor.)

Practice, practice, practice!

While practicing,
speak the words out loud.

Heel, Ball, Toe ~ Sway ….Repeat.

Resist the urge to look down at
your feet while practicing.

Now walk the talk!

Let's Go!

Day 2
2.0 Inch Mid-Heels:

Stay the course. Light and easy.

Your goal for Day 2 is a
½ hour of continuous wear.

(Preferably in the morning
on a tile floor.)

Speak the words out loud.

Heel, Ball, Toe ~ Sway ….Repeat.

Resist the urge to look down at
your feet while practicing.

Relax, breathe and remain calm!

Day 3
2.0 Inch Mid-Heels:

Double your wear time today!

Your goal for Day 3 is
1 hour of continuous wear.

Day 4
2.0 Inch Mid-Heels:

Rock steady. Continue on. . .

Your goal for today is
1 hour of continuous wear.

Day 5
2.0 Inch Mid-Heels:

It is time to double up. Let's go!

Your goal for today is
2 hours of continuous wear.

You will master
The Stiletto Glissade™.

Speak the words out loud,
Heel, Ball, Toe ~ Sway ….Repeat.

You're learning fast!

Well done!

Day 6
** 2.5 Inch Pre-Stilettos **

Increase your heel height today!
Inch your way up to a
2.5 Inch Pre-Stiletto.

Maintain your wear time.

Your goal for today is
2 hours of continuous wear.

Day 7
2.5 Inch Pre-Stilettos:

Remain focused.

Increase your wear time.

Your goal for today is
3 hours of continuous wear.

Day 8
2.5 Inch Pre-Stilettos:

Remain calm and continue to practice.

Today's goal is
3 hours of continuous wear.

Speak the words,
Heel, Ball, Toe ~ Sway ….Repeat.

Keep working on it!

Day 9
2.5 Inch Pre-Stilettos:

It's time to increase your wear time!

Your goal for today is
4 hours of continuous wear.

A special event or formal gala may consist of 4 hours of continuous wear.

Day 10
2.5 Inch Pre-Stilettos:

Maintain your wear time.
4 hours of continuous wear.

Congratulations!

Top Secret Operation: Step I Complete

Proficient
Pre-Stiletto Operative™

Day 11
★★ 3.0 Inch Stilettos ★★

<u>Today is the day</u> you step into the High Heights Universe!

Don your **3.0 Inch Stilettos** and walk into 4 hours of continuous wear!

Remember to take a Stiletto respite and carry your Stiletto satchel.

Let's Review
Top Secret Code:
The Stiletto Glissade™

Heel, Ball, Toe ~ Sway (HBTS). At the completion of your right great toe making contact with the surface of the floor, gently sway your pelvis to the right. At the completion of your left great toe making contact with the surface of the floor, gently sway your pelvis to the left.

Your head should be facing forward, with your chin slightly elevated. Shoulders down and slightly back, they should be in alignment with your pelvis. Your chest should be convex.

Your knees should be straight but not stiff or locked. Relax, breathe, and remain calm. Go!

Day 12
3.0 Inch Stilettos:

Continue to practice 4 hours of wear time in your 3.0 Inch Stilettos.

You're getting better everyday!

Day 13
3.0 Inch Stilettos:

Time to bump it up to
5 hours of continuous wear in your
3.0 Inch Stilettos.

Speak the words,
Heel, Ball, Toe ~Sway ….Repeat.

Day 14
3.0 Inch Stilettos:

Rock steady.

It's 5 hours of continuous wear today.

You're doing great!

Go!

Day 15
3.0 Inch Stilettos:

It's time to increase your wear time.

Your goal for today is
6 hours of continuous wear.

Remember to take a Stiletto respite
and carry your Stiletto satchel.

Day 16
3.0 Inch Stilettos:

Continue on...
6 hours of wear time today.

You will master
The Stiletto Glissade™.

Practice and speak the words,
Heel, Ball, Toe ~ Sway ....Repeat.

Outstanding!

You're doing very well!

Go!

Day 17
3.0 Inch Stilettos:

No turning back, full speed ahead.

Increase your wear time today.

7 hours of continuous wear.

Perseverance will pay off!

Let's Go Stiletto!™

Day 18
3.0 Inch Stilettos:

Remain calm and continue to practice.

7 hours of continuous wear today.

Speak the words,
Heel, Ball, Toe ~ Sway ….Repeat.

Remember to take a Stiletto respite and carry your Stiletto satchel.

Day 19
3.0 Inch Stilettos:

Today is the day to increase
your wear time.

Your goal for today is
8 hours of continuous wear.

A full day beauty seminar may consist
of 8 hours of continuous wear.

Practice, practice, practice!

Day 20
3.0 Inch Stilettos:

Maintain your wear time.
8 hours of continuous wear.

Congratulations!!

Top Secret Operation: Step II Complete

Professional Stiletto Operative™

"So let's not get tired of what is good. At just the right time we will reap a harvest of blessing if we don't give up."
Galatians 6:9

Day 21
★ 4.0 Inch Super Stilettos ★

It's time for that **Extra Inch!**

Don your **4.0 Inch Super Stilettos!**

Now that you are towering in 4.0 Inch Super Stilettos, <u>decrease</u> your wear time to 4 hours of continuous wear to allow for the adjustment to your new heel height.

Relax, breathe.
Remain Calm. Remain Focused.

Resist the urge to lean forward to balance yourself.

Remember to take a Stiletto respite and carry your Stiletto satchel.

Let's Review
Top Secret Code:
The Stiletto Glissade™

Heel, Ball, Toe ~ Sway (HBTS). At the completion of your right great toe making contact with the surface of the floor, gently sway your pelvis to the right. At the completion of your left great toe making contact with the surface of the floor, gently sway your pelvis to the left.

Your head should be facing forward, with your chin slightly elevated. Shoulders down and slightly back, they should be in alignment with your pelvis. Your chest should be convex. Your knees should be straight but not stiff or locked. Remember to take a Stiletto respite and carry your Stiletto satchel. Relax, breathe and remain calm.

Let's Go Stiletto!™

Day 22
4.0 Inch Super Stilettos:

Rock on with confidence.

4 hours of continuous wear today.

Keep up the good work!

Day 23
4.0 Inch Super Stilettos:

Time to bump it up to
5 hours of continuous wear in your
4.0 Inch Super Stilettos.

Speak the words,
Heel, Ball, Toe ~ Sway ….Repeat.

Day 24
4.0 Inch Super Stilettos:

Rock steady.

It's 5 hours of continuous wear today.

Remember to take a Stiletto respite and carry your Stiletto satchel.

Day 25
4.0 Inch Super Stilettos:

Yes, it's time to increase
your wear time.

Your goal for today is
6 hours of continuous wear.

Yes, you can!

Speak the words,
Heel, Ball, Toe ~ Sway ….Repeat.

Day 26
4.0 Inch Super Stilettos:

Continue to practice your
6 hours of wear time.

Day 27
4.0 Inch Super Stilettos:

You're going to make a
1 hour time leap today!

Your goal for today is
7 hours of continuous wear.

You will master
The Stiletto Glissade™.

Practice and speak the words,
Heel, Ball, Toe ~ Sway ....Repeat.

Relax, breathe.
Remain Calm. Remain Focused.

Let's Go Stiletto!™

Day 28
4.0 Inch Super Stilettos:

Continue to practice your
7 hours of continuous wear.

Remember to take a Stiletto respite
and carry your Stiletto satchel.

Days 29
4.0 Inch Super Stilettos:

Today is the day to
increase your wear time by 1 hour.

Rise up to 8 hours of continuous wear!

You're doing beautifully!

Day 30
4.0 Inch Super Stilettos:

Maintain your wear time.
8 hours of continuous wear!!!

Top Secret Operation: Step III Complete

Congratulations!!!
Mission Accomplished!!!

Precocious Stiletto Operative™

DIRECTIVE III

Stiletto Surveillance

Classified Stiletto Identities Revealed

The Stiletto is a master of disguises and has multiple identities for use on every cosmopolitan fashion mission. Some mission's call for the Stiletto to be covert, others call for her to be conspicuous. Each identity is carefully crafted to accomplish the mission for which she was designed.

The identity of the Stiletto is fluid. Her adaptation to her environment is quick and succinct. The versatility of the identity of the Stiletto lends to her greatness. She is forever changing and constantly evolving.

Stiletto Avowal

As a Proverbs 31 Woman, I vow to embrace each Classified Stiletto Identity while utilizing the correct Stiletto ambulation technique.

"Put on your new nature, and be renewed as you learn to know your Creator and become like him."
Colossians 3:10

"The king's heart is like a stream of water directed by the Lord; he guides it wherever he pleases."
Proverbs 21:1

Presidential Stiletto

Yes, Stilettos are indeed Presidential.

Not only does the Presidential Stiletto occupy The White House,

you will find her in Presidential Palaces and Royal Residences worldwide.

Hello Madam President!

Diplomatic Stiletto

Class and power embody the Diplomatic Stiletto. Do not touch. She has Diplomatic immunity. You will recognize her in a U.S. Embassy or at a State Dinner. Applause is required.

Regal Stiletto

The Regal Stiletto will be found dining with Presidents, Prime Ministers and Heads of State. At this moment, she is scripting power and grace at the highest level.

Elegant Stiletto

Nothing says class and elegance more finely than the Elegant Stiletto.

You will see the Elegant Stiletto at every dinner party and certainly at every white-tie event.

She represents a sense of stateliness and a degree of femininity that is unrivaled.

Powerful Stiletto

Power plus beauty, equals Stiletto. The Powerful Stiletto can change style decisions without warning. On purpose or subconsciously, she is taking charge right now, producing an environment conducive to supreme style engineering.

*"You are the God of great wonders!
You demonstrate your awesome power
among the nations."
Psalms 77:14*

Stunning Stiletto

Prepare to be amazed and enraptured by the Stunning Stiletto. By all accounts the Stunning Stiletto is superiorly impressive. She is perched atop a stage ready to stride with vigor and astound with beauty.

Womanly Stiletto

The Womanly Stiletto is the epitome of femininity. The Womanly Stiletto knows what to do to escalate or de-escalate a fashion drama situation. She sets the tone and commands the room. All eyes are on the Womanly Stiletto. . . at all times.

STILETTO DOSSIER

Mature Stiletto

The fully developed Mature Stiletto is for the mature woman.

The Mature Stiletto commands a level of self-confidence and assurance that comes with enlightenment that has been cultivated and developed throughout the ages.

Beautiful Stiletto

The Beautiful Stiletto is a wearable work of art while adorning the foot and extending the leg. She gives pleasure and delight to the beholder. The Beautiful Stiletto is exquisite in form and superb in function.

STILETTO DOSSIER

Influential Stiletto

The Influential Stiletto modifies how the wearer and the spectator expresses and interprets fashion. The Influential Stiletto is everlasting and relentless in her pursuit to anchor herself as an unmovable fashion figure.

"For God has not given us a spirit of fear and timidity, but of power, love, and self-discipline."
2 Timothy 1:7

Dynamic Stiletto

This Stiletto demands energy, vitality and action. The Dynamic Stiletto dares one to be subdued or reserved. Be Dynamic and don a Stiletto, Right now!

Ambitious Stiletto

The Ambitious Stiletto is proactive and positive in all of her fashion endeavors. The nature of the Ambitious Stiletto prompts her to zealously display an aura of peerless class and fashion dominance.

Creative Stiletto

The Creative Stiletto can create style where there is none. The Creative Stiletto has the ability to transform a fashion ensemble from mediocre to stunning in 5 seconds flat. Let's Go Stiletto!™

Exuberant Stiletto

The Exuberant Stiletto packs a powerful fashion punch and adds excitement to any fashion statement. This Stiletto is cheerful and full of energy. She will show up in an outlandish color combination and wow the crowd.

Prominent Stiletto

The Prominent Stiletto lends her authority to the authenticity of the entire fashion collaboration. There is no question this Stiletto will be the most Prominent fashion component one will don. She will never be overlooked or forgotten.

*"Be on guard. Stand firm in the faith.
Be courageous. Be strong."*
1 Corinthians 16:13

Daring Stiletto

The Daring Stiletto is not for the faint of heart. She is serious about style and fashion commentary. The Daring Stiletto dares to be uncommon without asking for permission to do so.

Marvelous Stiletto

Marvelous darling! Just Marvelous! Get ready to behold the Marvelous Stiletto as she graces the pages of high fashion magazines and blogs everywhere. The Marvelous Stiletto is never short on astonishment and has a plethora of puissance.

Resilient Stiletto

The Resilient Stiletto will bounce fashion from the outer court to the inner court of couture houses worldwide. This high spirited, sprightly Stiletto is clever enough to stage a fashion coup at 4pm and be on time for hors d'oeuvres at 6pm.

Important Stiletto

The Important Stiletto is crucial to authentic style. Fashion goes nowhere without the Important Stiletto. This Stiletto is so domineering, that without her, authentic high fashion

cannot exist.

Distinctive Stiletto

The Distinctive Stiletto is well respected, proper and notable. This Stiletto gives permission and credence to all other forms of fashion and is Chief among them.

"So be strong and courageous, all you who put your hope in the Lord!"
Psalms 31:24

Courageous Stiletto

It takes courage to don a Stiletto. The Courageous Stiletto is fearless and fierce. You must not allow her to overpower you. The Courageous Stiletto is for the sturdy, stalwart fashion maven.

Astounding Stiletto

The Astounding Stiletto is quite capable of overwhelming one with elation and euphoria. Prepare to be exhilarated by the style on the Astounding Stiletto.

Bold Stiletto

The Bold Stiletto roars loud with thunder and rebukes timidity. This Stiletto is bodacious and treads intrepidly. She is gutsy and does not ask for the opinion of the spectator.

Liberating Stiletto

Freedom through fashion!

The Liberating Stiletto gives you the freedom to explore multiple fashion possibilities. She releases freedom from preconceived fashion dictatorships and allows new style to emerge and be heard.

Fascinating Stiletto

The Fascinating Stiletto piques ones curiosity, prompting the stare with amazement effect. This Stiletto causes one to be transfixed with her irresistible attraction. She is alluring at all times and absolutely refuses to be boring.

The Proverbs 31 Woman

"She is clothed with strength and dignity, and she laughs without fear of the future."
Proverbs 31:25

STILETTO DOSSIER

Adventurous Stiletto

Take a leap up and come out of your safety zone. Don an Adventurous Stiletto. The Adventurous Stiletto is zany and fun loving. She is a pioneer and travails on the edge of fashion acceptability.

Intense Stiletto

The Intense Stiletto is red hot and full of fervid style. She is packing some heat, setting off all alarms and will not be extinguished.

Step it up a notch!

Let's Go Stiletto!™

Brawny Stiletto

The Brawny Stiletto is the strength beneath your feet. She breathes easy while supporting your frame with style, elevating your status with distinction and extending your legs with luxury.

Amazing Stiletto

The Amazing Stiletto dives right into impromptu color and style without hesitation. This Stiletto is a phenomenon. She can and does forecast and foreshadow her own style success.

Delightful Stiletto

Donning a Stiletto is Delightful. Be Delighted to be in your Stiletto and she will respond to you in kind. The Delightful Stiletto is cleverly congenial and totally generous with style.

*"Take delight in the Lord, and he will
give you your heart's desires."
Psalms 37:4*

Engaging Stiletto

The Engaging Stiletto draws an audience without effort. She engages the spectator in an atmosphere of style, elegance and beauty.

Staring is required!

Befitting Stiletto

The Befitting Stiletto is fit for a Queen.

That's you!

We are all royalty in the eyes of God.

Do not ever de-value yourself.

Don a Befitting Stiletto and walk as if you are always wearing a diadem.

Resolute Stiletto

The Resolute Stiletto is absolutely determined to be seen and heard. She makes a bold, irrevocable fashion proclamation, which is a testament to her Resolute power.

All rise!

Spontaneous Stiletto

The unpredictability of this Stiletto is part of her fashion success. The Spontaneous Stiletto stages style soirees daily at 6pm, then instantly walks into the role of guest of honor.

Social Stiletto

The Social Stiletto is outgoing and gregarious. She is an icebreaker and conversation starter. The Social Stiletto is friendly, cozy and effortlessly forthcoming about her global fashion governance.

"Shout joyful praises to God, all the earth!"
Psalms 66:1

International Stiletto

The International Stiletto cannot be contained in one country. Her fashion prowess jumps oceans and transverses continents. Her appearance alone mesmerizes her audience.

Successful Stiletto

The Successful Stiletto has been relevant for decades and will continue to grace us with her benevolent presence for many years to come. The Successful Stiletto has infinite staying power and style durability.

Energetic Stiletto

The Energetic Stiletto is upbeat and high-spirited. She stands at the ready to serve as the answer to every fashion equation. This Stiletto has the stamina to stand tall and she always delivers.

Historical Stiletto

The Historical Stiletto is a style curator that never fails to share fashion from her archives on a daily basis. She specializes in the classic as well as the cutting edge.

Magnificent Stiletto

The Magnificent Stiletto shines forth forebodingly. This Stiletto is empowered to make an imposing statement. She embraces sublimity and freely gives loveliness.

"Thank you for making me so wonderfully complex! Your workmanship is marvelous — how well I know it."
Psalms 139:14

Glamorous Stiletto

This Stiletto knows Glamour from top to bottom and side to side. She is a runway walker and red carpet talker. The Glamorous Stiletto always occupies the VIP suite and is under constant surveillance by the paparazzi.

Rich Stiletto

This Stiletto is Rich in history, class and elegance. The Rich Stiletto carries with her, decades of style, humility and character. The wealth of style on this Stiletto is matchless.

Splendid Stiletto

The Splendid Stiletto is luxurious in all of her nobility. She is grandiose and sumptuous. The Splendid Stiletto gives rise to a star-studded symmetrical style performance, with daily encores.

Extraordinary Stiletto

The Extraordinary Stiletto is miles and miles away from mediocre or average. This Stiletto forcefully demonstrates mind-boggling style without mercy. She is noteworthy and remarkable.

Fierce Stiletto

The Fierce Stiletto resides on the sharp edge of fashion and is eager for style sovereignty. She will cut out her style niche quickly, without a second thought or a look back.

Let's Go Stiletto!™

"O Lord, our Lord, your majestic name fills the earth! Your glory is higher than the heavens."
Psalms 8:1

Spectacular Stiletto

The Spectacular Stiletto is a dramatic showstopper. She does not hold back her ravishing desire to unleash super savvy sagacious style.

Gorgeous Stiletto

The Gorgeous Stiletto is superb in her grandeur. She shimmers at all the right times and is known for being stop and stare Gorgeous. The time is now for her to rise and shine.

Sparkling Stiletto

The Sparkling Stiletto is a gem with many facets. This Stiletto presents glitz and glam galore. She adapts extremely well to her environment and is culturally acclimated with universal appeal.

Different Stiletto

The Different Stiletto holds her own unique place in the fashion world. She dictates, dominates and commands where fashion is going. The Different Stiletto is highly peculiar and displays exemplary style.

Witty Stiletto

The Witty Stiletto always has something canny to say.
She is outspoken, forthright and bold.
This Stiletto is cleverly dictating her fashion manifesto.
Stop, look and listen.

The Proverbs 31 Woman

"When she speaks, her words are wise, and she gives instructions with kindness."
Proverbs 31:26

Timeless Stiletto

The Timeless Stiletto is fashion memorabilia from the past and fashion treasure for the future.

Her classic fashion preeminence will never expire.

Sporty Stiletto

The Sporty Stiletto is stylishly appropriate for attending a tennis match, golf tourney or jazz concert in the amphitheatre. She is a light, airy, breezy winner.

Sophisticated Stiletto

The Sophisticated Stiletto is well versed in cultures around the world. The Sophisticated Stiletto knows what to say in Rome and in Roanoke. Watch and learn.

Luxurious Stiletto

Ahhh... the Luxurious Stiletto!

She is opulent and prosperous.

Her movements are fluid and graceful.

The Luxurious Stiletto enjoys fine living and compliments every refined environment.

Pretty Stiletto

The Pretty Stiletto is aesthetically pleasing. She approaches style in a subtle manner, yet does not downplay the seriousness of her prettiness.

She offers up a daily portion of mesmeric beauty served on a platter.

"But true wisdom and power are found in God; counsel and understanding are his."
Job 12:13

Intelligent Stiletto

This Stiletto charts the course for style intelligence. The Intelligent Stiletto understands what is required to carry out a well-organized, highly innovative fashion takeover.

Stately Stiletto

At this very moment, the Stately Stiletto is making her grand entrance into a castle, palace or private jet. The Stately Stiletto is ceremonial and she brings with her bejeweled regalia.

Alive Stiletto

This Stiletto is alive, well and kicking. She embraces life, luxury, liberty and the pursuit of happiness. Her celebratory style comes alive with each step.

Let's Go Stiletto!™

Renowned Stiletto

The Renowned Stiletto is known for her ability to unveil, cultivate and enhance any style composition. She is the adhesive that binds together individual style sentences into one cohesive well-spoken fashion statement.

STILETTO DOSSIER

Glistening Stiletto

Glitter, glam and glow, Oh my! The Glistening Stiletto allows her fashion fullness to catch every flash of light and glow bright. The high lights on this Stiletto remain on at all times.

"Wisdom will multiply your days and add years to your life."
Proverbs 9:11

Brilliant Stiletto

Curtains up! The Brilliant Stiletto is ready to take center stage. This Stiletto is a illustrious, super talented performance professional.
She delights in being in the spotlight.

Dangerous Stiletto

Only the fashion maverick wears the Dangerous Stiletto. She is highly stylish and unpredictable. The Dangerous Stiletto is distinctive and drives high fashion right over the edge.

Brave Stiletto

The Brave Stiletto is a bold and brave fashion artisan. She is for the fashion champion, the style warrior.

The Brave Stiletto navigates her own path through uncharted territory.

Educated Stiletto

The Educated Stiletto has precise insight on all things fashionable and decorative. She has a master's degree in high fashion and a surplus of experience in style expression.

Lively Stiletto

Step Lively! This Stiletto is filled with strength and vigor. The Lively Stiletto is readily available to leap out onto the stage of life and perform. She dances with excitement daily.

"God is my strong fortress, and he makes my way perfect."
2 Samuel 22:33

STILETTO DOSSIER

Victorious Stiletto

This Stiletto is not only Victorious, but valiant as well. The Victorious Stiletto is a winner and always prevails over fashion failures. She is unrestrained and raring to go.

Happy Stiletto

This Stiletto is happy and overjoyed.

The Happy Stiletto flawlessly orchestrates the coming together of sole and soul.

She is fruitful, fitting and giddy.

Outstanding Stiletto

The Outstanding Stiletto never recoils from attention. This Stiletto takes a prominent position on the podium, strikes a pose for all to behold and delivers without an introduction.

Wealthy Stiletto

The Wealthy Stiletto is affluent and owns resources untold. She controls the key to a vault full of style, class and grace. The Wealthy Stiletto has a storehouse full of global style currency.

Affable Stiletto

The Affable Stiletto is always civil, approachable and cordial. She is a well-mannered guest at every dinner party. The Affable Stiletto makes her presence known without ever overshadowing the host.

"Always be joyful."
1 Thessalonians 5:16

Pleasant Stiletto

The Pleasant Stiletto is benevolent and courteous. She just happens to be well versed in social etiquette and ceremonial manners. The Pleasant Stiletto pays attention to detail and abides by decorum and protocol.

Fearless Stiletto

Fearless Baby! This Stiletto is Fearless. The Fearless Stiletto can quash a fashion fiasco quickly without backup from the fashion enforcement squad. The runway of life is calling and she answers the call without hesitation or fear.

Caring Stiletto

The Caring Stiletto cares not about gentle fashion expression. She cares about dominating the fashion world, one step at a time. The Caring Stiletto fosters style invention and nurtures style predominance.

Classy Stiletto

The Classy Stiletto transcends time. She is ageless and ravishing.

The Classy Stiletto is always recognized by spectators, due to her dedication to timeless exquisite style.

Gleaming Stiletto

The Gleaming Stiletto shimmers where others leave a shadow. She stars in her own parade and rides high into exclusive fashion houses everywhere.

The Proverbs 31 Woman

"There are many virtuous and capable women in the world, but you surpass them all!"
Proverbs 31:29

STILETTO DOSSIER

Astonishing Stiletto

Prepare to be Astonished by this Stiletto. The Astonishing Stiletto is a powerhouse of perfect form and grace. She is breathtaking at every turn and delivers the unexpected with striking precision.

Encouraging Stiletto

This Stiletto encourages style to be unrestrained and released from restrictions. The Encouraging Stiletto fortifies self-expression and style supremacy.

STILETTO DOSSIER

Wonderful Stiletto

The Wonderful Stiletto is jaw dropping and awe-inspiring. She will spontaneously command a standing ovation and happily deliver an encore appearance.

Profound Stiletto

The Profound Stiletto has the ability to dictate style, exude confidence and gracefully command attention, all at the same time.

Immense Stiletto

The Immense Stiletto is large and in charge. She packs some colossal style and exudes monumental magnificence.

"Anyone who loves another brother or sister is living in the light and does not cause others to stumble."
1 John 2:10

Righteous Stiletto

The Righteous Stiletto is honest and upright. She is audacious and unapologetic. The Righteous Stiletto upholds style integrity and is sterling in her style endeavors.

Elated Stiletto

The Elated Stiletto is ecstatic about style. She is overjoyed, jubilant and delighted to be the Fashion Director of your entire Stiletto collection.

Fabulous Stiletto

Stilettos *ARE* Fabulous!

The Fabulous Stiletto tells a fabulous true tale about being the fashion Queen-pin of the world!

Vital Stiletto

The Vital Stiletto is a breath of fresh air. The survival of style depends on her. She has been known to cause an increased pulse rate and goo-goo eyes in the beholder.

Coherent Stiletto

The Coherent Stiletto makes perfect sense. She is lucid, articulate and reasonable. This Stiletto is the logical choice for the fashion connoisseur.

*"Your word is a lamp to guide my feet
and a light for my path."
Psalms 119:105*

Essential Stiletto

The Essential Stiletto is quite necessary, in fact, indispensable. She is crucial, capable and highly recognizable as the quintessential style tool.

Radiant Stiletto

Radiance galore, need I say more! The Radiant Stiletto is incandescent, sunny and bright. She ushers in well-rehearsed style and classical dignity.

Serious Stiletto

The Serious Stiletto is deliberate and determined, steadfast and provocative. This Stiletto is very selective in her style promotion. She speaks loud and clear and refuses to be silent.

Convivial Stiletto

The Convivial Stiletto is fun loving and festive. She is cheerful with every turn. The Convivial Stiletto is ready for an afternoon on Broadway or a night out on the town.

Generous Stiletto

This Stiletto freely gives fashion sense. The Generous Stiletto is philanthropic in her venture to offer up compassion with kindness that is priceless.

*"Great is his faithfulness; his mercies
begin afresh each morning."
Lamentations 3:23*

Stupendous Stiletto

The Stupendous Stiletto steps on stage ready to perform and captivate her audience. She quickly digests all the accolades and attention she receives and then simply asks for more.

Desired Stiletto

The Desired Stiletto embodies a full dose of femininity, which guarantees her desirability. She causes the spectator to pine for one last glance of her greatness.

STILETTO DOSSIER

Lavish Stiletto

The Lavish Stiletto is over the top in style and luxury. She makes no apologies for excess and extravagance. More importantly, she relishes in Queenly grandeur.

Famous Stiletto

This Stiletto is notorious for quickly dismantling a fashion faux pas. The Famous Stiletto is legendary for her ability to positively rearrange a fashion situation. She is preceded by her virtuous reputation.

Cultured Stiletto

The Cultured Stiletto has her own time machine and is able to walk back through time and forward through culture, with grace and style. She speaks of international erudition and respected individuality.

"You are altogether beautiful, my darling, beautiful in every way."
Song of Songs 4:7

Iconic Stiletto

The Iconic Stiletto is a walking historian. She serves as a testament to the Iconic nature of the Stiletto, as introduced in the old world movie star era of the 1950's and 60's. This Iconic glamorous imagery, inclusive of the Stiletto, continues today on the red carpets of Hollywood and throughout the world.

DIRECTIVE IV

Stiletto Rescue & Recovery

Status Post
Mission Accomplished

Congratulations on the successful completion of this Top Secret Mission. Utilizing the correct Stiletto ambulation technique, The Stiletto Glissade™, is essential to accurately reflect your true **image** as a Proverbs 31 Woman.

The **image** you convey, by the manner in which you walk, is how you are perceived, received and interpreted. Continue to walk in Stilettos with grace through **faith**.

Your audience is waiting. Walk in **faith** and illuminate with each step. Let's Go Stiletto!™

Stiletto SOS
Save Our Soles

Not every Stiletto will be suitable for ambulation due to the height of the heel, the fit or design. No discomposure or abashment should be felt by choosing to don Stilettos that are for display only (FDO). Carry your FDO Stilettos with you in your Stiletto satchel or conspicuously dangle your FDO Stilettos by the first two fingers on one hand. Wait until you are seated to put them on or let them pose neatly next to your feet. If your actions cause any unusually long stares from spectators, give them a subtle smile and the parade wave.

Top Secret Opulence:
Restoration

Relax, breathe and elevate your feet. Treat your feet with kindness and luxury. Create a Restoration Station in your home, a designated space for rest and relaxation, complete with a chaise longue and mini-fridge. Lavish your feet with opulent foot care emollients. Invest in a foot spa, as well as, plush slippers, socks and pillows for your feet.

Assign time for bi-weekly pedicures. In addition to pedicures see a professional masseuse for lower leg and foot massages. Remove any visible hair from your great toe and other areas of your feet. Inspect your feet daily for potential health concerns, including poor circulation, helomata (corns) and calluses. See your podiatrist at regularly scheduled intervals.

Stiletto Avowal

As a Proverbs 31 Woman, I vow to engage in Top Secret Opulence by loving myself and caring for myself with affection and dedication.

"Love never gives up, never loses faith, is always hopeful, and endures through every circumstance."
1 Corinthians 13:7

Soul Salvation
Save Our Souls

"If you confess with your mouth that Jesus is Lord and believe in your heart that God raised him from the dead, you will be saved."
Romans 10:9

Prayer of Salvation

Father God,

I come to you in the name of Jesus Christ. I admit that I am a sinner. I repent of my sins and ask for your forgiveness. I believe that your Son Jesus Christ died for my sins, has risen, and is now seated at your right hand. I accept Jesus Christ as my Lord and Savior and according to your word, I am saved. Lord Jesus, send your Holy Spirit to transform my life so that I may faithfully serve you and bring glory to your name.

Amen

Stiletto Disclaimer

While the author and publisher have used their best efforts in preparing this book, they make no representations with respect to the accuracy or completeness of the contents of this book and specifically disclaim any implied warranties.

The material contained herein is for general information purposes only and does not constitute advice of any kind. In addition, the author does not claim ownership of the heel, ball and toe motion, as this method of walking is a normal gait pattern used for locomotion. The phrase, The Stiletto Glissade™, is the trademarked property of the author, as well as other terms or phrases where the trademark(™) symbol is indicated.

The author, publisher and all affiliates accept no responsibility and exclude all liability in connection with the use or application of the information contained herein. Any reference to websites, books or other reference material does not constitute or imply endorsement.

Notes

[1] Dagger. (n.d.). Online Etymology Dictionary. Retrieved July 1, 2012, from http://dictionary.reference.com/browse/dagger

[2] New Living Translation Bible Verses.

[3] Pringle, C. (2004). *Roger Vivier*. New York, NY: Assouline.

[4] Semmelhack, E. (2008). *Heights of fashion: A history of the elevated shoe*. Toronto, Ontario, Canada: Gutenberg Periscope.

[5] Stiletto. (n.d.). Online Etymology Dictionary. Retrieved July 1, 2012, from http://dictionary.reference.com/browse/Stiletto

ABOUT THE AUTHOR

C.C. Preston, M.S., is a Stilettologist, Stiletto Ambulation Coach and Social Etiquette Educator.

www.ingramcontent.com/pod-product-compliance
Lightning Source LLC
Chambersburg PA
CBHW031640040426
42453CB00006B/168